Sandra Bosnic

Bookpresentation: "Slumdog Millionaire" by Vikas Swarup and comparison with movie

GRIN Publishing

Bibliographic information published by the German National Library:

The German National Library lists this publication in the National Bibliography; detailed bibliographic data are available on the Internet at http://dnb.dnb.de .

Imprint:

Copyright © 2011 GRIN Verlag, Open Publishing GmbH
Print and binding: Books on Demand GmbH, Norderstedt Germany
ISBN: 978-3-656-22764-9

This book at GRIN:

http://www.grin.com/en/e-book/191507/bookpresentation-slumdog-millionaire-by-vikas-swarup-and-comparison

The plot:

"I have been arrested. For winning a quiz show."[7]

This is the sentence the tale starts with. The orphan boy Ram Mohammad Thomas got arrested for winning the biggest quiz-show in India called "Who Will Win a Billion?" (W3B). The police took him into prison on suspicion of cheating and he got tortured. They wanted him to confess that he cheated although he didn't. The real reason for his capture was that the company W3B didn't have the money to pay him and so they misquoted him to cheat. Ram Mohammad Thomas didn't go to school and was a poor boy. He grew up in Dharavi, one of the biggest slums in the world. Smita Shah, his lawyer, rescued him from being tortured. She heard about the unbelievable story of the street child winning one billion Rupees at W3B and about his arrest. So she went into prison, although she told him she didn't know him. Both watched the quiz-show on DVD and Ram explains her in short flashbacks 12 stories of his turbulent life, which helped him to answer all the questions in the correct way. At last it comes out that Smita is a girl he lived next to when he was a teenager. Her real name is Gudiya and he saved her from her alcoholic father. Smita fought for his right and at last he got his prize. He needs the money to pay Nita's pimp, so she has no longer to work as a prostitute. In the end they got married.

Important topics the book deals with:

- Slums in India

Dharavi is a suburb of Mumbai and actually one of the largest slums in the world. More than 1 million people live there on an area about 175 hectares. Mumbai is a rich city with its big Bollywood movie industry but their inhabitants try to ignore the problems in the slums located next to them. In the book Ram thinks after his arrest:

"There are those who will say that I brought this upon myself. By dabbling in that quiz show. They will wag a finger at me and remind me of what the elders in Dharavi say about never crossing the dividing line that separates the rich from the poor."[8]

And he also explains that no one cares about if somebody gets arrested or disappears because people have to fight for their own existence. In fact the population living there are illegal and the cots built there are as well. That is the reason for having no running-water and much to few sanitary installations. Dharavi slum has developed because humans from poor villages wanted to start a better life in Mumbai. Since Mumbai is too expensive, these people have to rent a cot in Dharavi. Many children go begging and men work as day-worker. However they say living there is still better than in the village where they came from.

- caste system in India

The cast system belongs to the Hinduism. Humans get born into one cast and have to stay in this separate community of people. If they live a decent life, they get reborn into the next higher caste after death. Ram belongs to the group of "Sudras" because he works as a waiter.

- religions in India

As Ram was set out in front of a church by his mother on the day he was born, nobody knew which religion his parents believed in. So the priest decided to give him three names, each one standing for another religion.

Ram	- stands for the Hindusim
Mohammad	- stands for the Islam
Thomas	- stands for the Christianity

India has different religions, about 82% Hindu, 11% muslim and 2,5% Christian population. The remaining religions are 1% Buddism, 0,5% Jains and some Jewish inhabitants. Due to that there are often tensions in the population.

---

[7] „Slumdog Millionaire" page 1
[8] „Slumdog Millionaire" page 3

"What I discovered after receiving the payout was that with money I had power even over the police"[10]

Taking bribe money is another important problem in India. According to the population in Delhi the following funds must be paid:

- In order to get off as traffic offender: $ 2 - 10
- For the distribution of a passport: $ 2
- For the permission of a private passenger car: $ 1,000
- For the punctual supply of drinking water by urban authorities: $ 2 - 4 / week

There are many humans, who must get along in India with less than 1.25 dollar a day

Most important differences between the book and the movie:

book	movie
The main character is called Ram Mohammad Thomas	The main character is called Jamal Malik
Salim is his best friend and becomes a Bollywood actor.	Salim is his brother and a criminal
Ram's big love is a prostitute called Nita, he got to know her at the age of 13	Jamal's big love is Latika and he has known her since childhood.
Ram is an orphan boy who grew up with a priest. He never knew his mother.	Jamal is a street child and his mother was killed in local riots between Muslims and Hindus.
Ram went to W3B because he wanted to take revenge on Prem Kumar, the host of the show, because he injured Nita very badly and he needs money to pay Nita's pimp to get her free.	Jamal went to W3B because he hopes Latika would watch him and he will meet her again.
Ram tells the hole story of his life to his lawyer Smita.	Jamal tells the story to the cop, who tortured him.
He wins 1 billion rupees.	He wins 20 million rupees.

Own opinion:

The book pleased me very well, since it is variedly written and you can imagine yourself well into the story. In addition to that I learned many interesting facts about India. Which pleased me also very well, is the fact that all bad humans in the tale got what they deserved and the story has a happy ending. The book is exciting and I can definitely recommend it. In my opinion the book is much better than the film, since so many topics in the film were not addressed and the story has been completely changed.

Vocab:

traffic offender = Verkehrssünder	riot = Aufstand, Unruhe	pimp = Zuhälter
torture = Folter	day-worker = Tagelöhner	
capture = Verhaftung	(to) dabble in = sich als/ in etwas versuchen	
bribe money = Bestechungsgeld	urban authorities = städt. Behörden	
cot = Wellblechhütte	juvenile = Jugend / kindisch	

Sources:
http://edition.cnn.com/video/#/video/world/2009/02/22/sidner.india.slumdog.inspiration.cnn?iref=videosearch (last access: 22-11-2011 20:27)
http://destination-asien.de/indien/religion.htm (last access: 12-11-11 22:23)
http://www.vikasswarup.net/index_files/Page607.htm (last access: 06-11-2011 18:05)
Picture Vikas Swarup: http://www.kiwi-verlag.de/ifiles/autor/big/autor_1023.jpg (last access: 22.11.11 - 21:11)

[9] http://www.zeit.de/2011/36/Indien-Anna-Hazare (last access: 22-11-2011 20:33)
[10] Slumdog Millionaire, page 216

„Hole in the wall project" in India

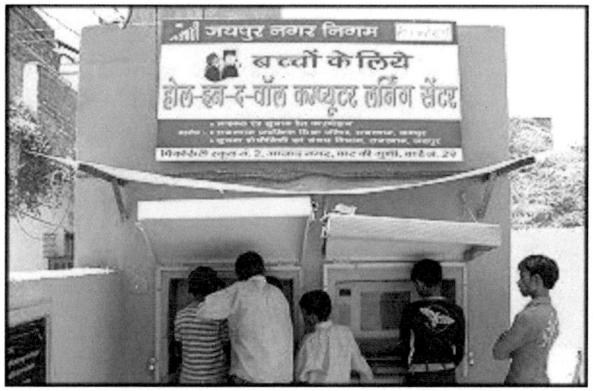

Caste system in India

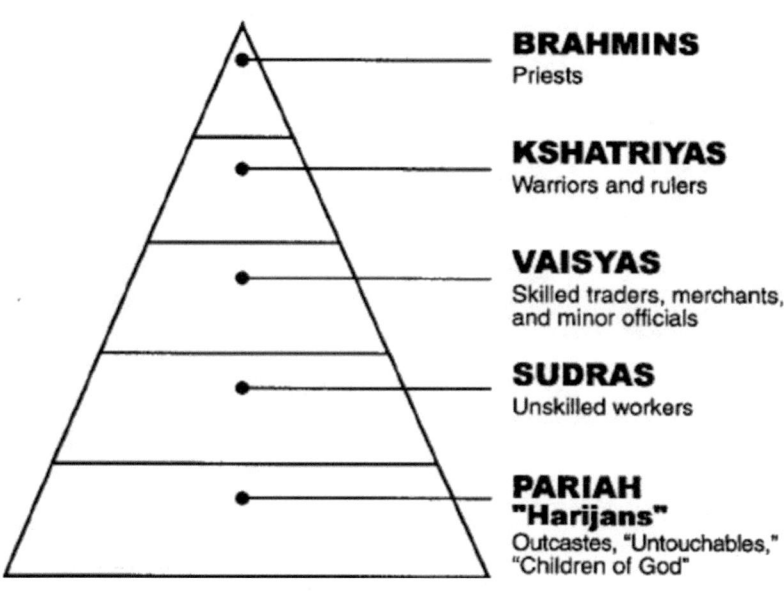

BRAHMINS
Priests

KSHATRIYAS
Warriors and rulers

VAISYAS
Skilled traders, merchants,
and minor officials

SUDRAS
Unskilled workers

**PARIAH
"Harijans"**
Outcastes, "Untouchables,"
"Children of God"

Main characters:

11

Nita

- works as a prostitute

12

Ram M. Thomas

13

Salim

no picture

Nita's brother

- he is her pimp

14

Prem Kumar

- Quiz-show-master

15

Smita

- She is Ram's lawyer

	India
Hindu	**82.0 %**
Muslim	**11.0 %**
Christian	**2.5 %**
Sikh	**1.9 %**
Buddhist	**1.0 %**
None	**0.0 %**

Top Religions in India

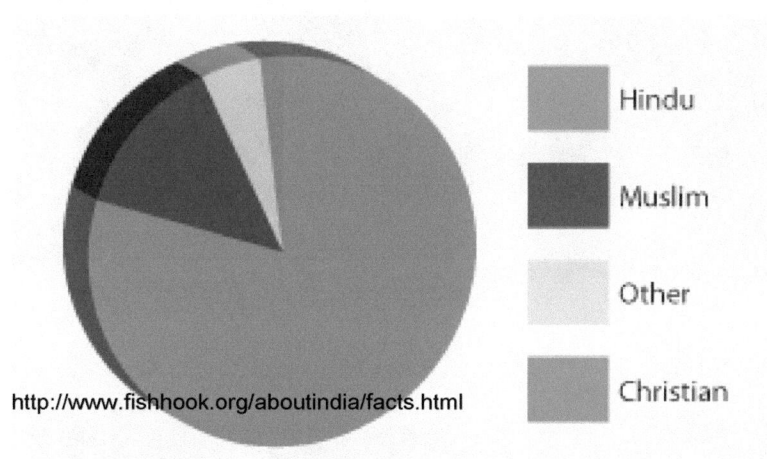

http://www.fishhook.org/aboutindia/facts.html

corruption in India

Taking bribe money is another important problem in India. According to the population Delhi the following funds must be paid:

- In order to get off as traffic offender: $ 2 - 10
- For the distribution of a passport: $ 2
- For the permission of a private passenger car: $ 1,000
- For the punctual supply of drinking water by urban authorities: $ 2 - 4 /
  week

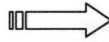

There are many humans, who must get along with less than 1.25 dollar a day

Dharavi Slum

http://s.ngm.com/2007/05/dharavi-mumbai-slum/img/dharavi-industry-615.jpg

http://farm2.static.flickr.com/1076/1407245592_68379a0b99.jpg

Most important differences between the book and the movie:

book	movie
The main character is called Ram Mohammad Thomas	The main character is called Jamal Malik
Salim is his best friend and becomes a Bollywood actor.	Salim is his brother and a criminal
Ram's big love is a prostitute called Nita, he got to know her at the age of 13	Jamal's big love is Latika and he has known her since childhood.
Ram is an orphan boy who grew up with a priest. He never knew his mother.	Jamal is a street child and his mother was killed in local riots between Muslims and Hindus.
Ram went to W3B because he wanted to take revenge on Prem Kumar, the host of the show, because he injured Nita very badly and he needs money to pay Nita's pimp to get her free.	Jamal went to W3B because he hopes Latika would watch him and he will meet her again.
Ram tells the hole story of his life to his lawyer Smita.	Jamal tells the story to the cop, who tortured him.
He wins 1 billion rupees.	He wins 20 million rupees.

Book presentation: Slumdog millionaire

- The author: Vikas Swarup

- His inspiration for the story

- About the book:

- Main characters of the book

- The plot

- Important topics the book deals with:

- Slums in India

- Caste system in India

- Religions in India

- Corruption in India

- Most important differences between the book and the movie

- Own opinion

- Vocab

Book presentation: Slumdog millionaire

The author: Vikas Swarup

- He was born in Allahabad in India, his parents were lawyers
- He has studied history, psychology and philosophy at Allahabad University
- Joined the Indian Foreign Service in 1986 and visited various countries
- Since 2009 he is Consul General of India in Osaka-Kobe, Japan
- He did his doctorate in literature & philosophy
- He also works as a writer for many international well-known magazines

His inspiration for the story:

Vikas Swarup was inspired by a project in India called "Hole in the wall project". It is about computers set up into a wall in poor areas of the world and also in Dhraravi slum. Children have the opportunity to teach themselves how to work on a computer and to communicate with each other. Using the computers with internet access is for free.

About the book:

The novel Slumdog Millionaire was originally published called "q&a" (= "questions and answers"). It was Vikas Swarup's first book. After publishing it in 2005, "q&a" became very popular. The book has been translated into 42 languages and won different awards, such as "Best First Book by the Commonwealth Writers's Prize" in 2006, "Most Influential Book of 2008" in Taiwan, "Best Travel Read in 2009".

An audio book and a film titled "Slumdog millionaire" were published in addition to the book. Both won also many awards, especially the movie won four Golden Globes and eight Oscars.

Main characters of the book:

Nita	Ram M. Thomas	Salim	Prem Kumar	Smita
She is a prostitute Ram falls in love with. Her brother is her pimp. To get her free Ram has to pay a lot of money.	He is the main character and participant in a quiz show. He loves Nita.	He is Ram's best friend and he wants to become a Bollywood-star.	He is the quiz-show-master and he injured Nita very bad after having sex with her.	She is Ram's lawyer. In the end it comes out that Ram saved her from her alcoholic father when she was a child. Her real name is Gudiya.

1 http://www.kiwi-verlag.de/ifiles/autor/big/autor_1023.jpg
2 http://medien.filmreporter.de/images/thumbnails/22174_200.jpg (last access: 19-11-2011 16:43)
3 http://www.nilacharal.com/enter/celeb/images/dev_patel.jpg (last access: 22-11-2011 20:46)
4 http://static.eventful.com/images/movieposter127by190/celebrities/518409/518409_v4_ba.jpg (last access: 22-11-2011 20:51)
5 http://3.bp.blogspot.com/_Ee5MXpRtZjA/SitpS7JyEPI/AAAAAAAAAZ4/vzqbjk5mR9I/s400/anil_kapoor145.jpg (22-11-11 21:00)
6 http://2.bp.blogspot.com/_nFudr-Whonw/TEpzkWeUyUI/AAAAAAAAI0g/Ofsndu6AJ9w/s1600/pop-singer-smita-stills-at-events-5.jpg (last access: 22-11-